WORKING LIVES

The Coal Mines

Nathaniel Harris

B T BATSFORD LTD   LONDON

F

Dedicaton
To my friends George Hardy and Stuart Phillips

Typeset by Tek-Art Ltd, Kent
and printed in Great Britain by
R.J. Acford
Chichester, Sussex
for the publishers
B.T. Batsford Ltd,
4 Fitzhardinge Street,
London W1H 0AH

ISBN 0 7134 5097 5

Frontispiece
*Hewing coal. In Britain, coal was 'hand got' in some
places until quite recent times.*

Cover illustrations
*The colour photograph shows a modern coal cutter in
action at Daw Mill Colliery, Coventry (National Coal
Board); the black and white photograph shows a
pillar and stall mine in Staffordshire; the portrait is of
Jack Fisher, a miner at the Chislet Colliery at
Canterbury (BBC Hulton Picture Library).*

Acknowledgments
The Author and Publishers would like to thank the
following for their kind permission to reproduce
copyright photographs: BBC Hulton Picture Library for
figures 22, 40, 41, 47 and 48; Beamish North of England
Open Air Museum for figures 18, 20, 24, 29, 31, 35, 36, 38
and 39; National Coal Board for figures 7, 8, 14, 43, 44
and 45; National Museum of Labour History for figures
6, 9, 11, 26 and 37; The Science Museum for figures 3,
10, 12, 15 and 16; The Times for figures 49 and 50;
Topham for figure 42. The pictures were researched
by Ros Morris.
   The Author would like to give his special thanks to all
the miners past and present who contributed their
memories to this book.

21118041 $\mathbb{I}$

TS

Contents

List of Illustrations

1 The Growth of the Coal Industry

Beginnings

Miners have been at work in Britain since prehistoric times, digging for flint, tin, lead, iron and even gold. On this time-scale, the coal industry is a relatively recent development. For centuries, coal must have seemed one of the more useless gifts of nature: who needed a smokey, dirty fuel, buried in the ground, when Britain was covered with dense forests offering firewood for the taking? In ancient times only the Romans in the north of England and in Wales used coal at all; and after the collapse of Roman Britain the Anglo-Saxons, who conquered and settled in England, ignored it completely. Some years after the Norman Conquest of 1066, King William ordered a complete record to be made of his kingdom's resources, and this – the famous Domesday Book – does not so much as mention coal.

Over the next few hundred years, coal began to be mined on a very small scale in many places; easily the most important, then and for centuries to come, was Tyneside on the north-east coast of England. The main users were smiths and lime-burners, but most people continued to regard coal as a public nuisance. From Queen Eleanor in the thirteenth century to the painter Nicholas Hilliard in the sixteenth, the 'sulfirous ayres' created by coal-burners were a source of irritation; Hilliard even claimed that they could spoil an artist's colours. As late as 1554 a Venetian envoy to England observed that:

In the North, towards Scotland, they find a sort of earth, almost mineral, which burns like char-coal and is extensively used by blacksmiths. But for the bad odour it leaves, it would be yet more employed, since it gives great heat and costs little.

The envoy's report soon became out of date. During the reign of Queen Elizabeth (1558-1603), industry and trade expanded dramatically and, as the forests were cut down and timber supplies dwindled, there was a particularly heavy demand for coal. London, already a city with several hundred thousand inhabitants, became dependent for its domestic and industrial fuel on coal shipped from Newcastle; the English road system was so bad that it was quicker and safer to transport goods by water, and so 'sea coal' turned Newcastle into a major port.

London had become a sooty city by the early seventeenth century, but the installation of proper chimneys in many houses got rid of the worst fumes from coal fires indoors. As a popular fuel, coal boomed throughout the seventeenth and eighteenth centuries, benefiting from population growth and economic expansion. In turn, coal production advanced economic growth and stimulated the development of new technology: the earliest practicable steam engines were designed for pumping, to cope with flooding in mines, and at Newcastle the first 'railways' were installed – fixed rails along which men or horses could haul waggons.

Working in early coal mines

Much early mining was primitive and amateurish.

HUMBERLAND

BR

Green Cot
Bridge
Plessy Hall
Plessy
Blyth
Lark Hall
Shank
Strickley
Lyesdon
Hartley New Harbour or Seaton Sluice

Sir M.W. Ridley Bart
Blagdon
Cramlington
Down Hill
Sir Jn Seaton Bart
Lord Delaval Seaton Delaval
Third Obelisk
Whitridge
New Putt
Hartley
Hartley
St Marys or Bates I.

Prestwick Car
Seaton
Burn
Satghill
Ruins
Burraden
Backworth
Earsden
Fenwick Esqr
Holywell
White Cot

Ethend Hall
Dinnington
Prestwick
Woolsington
Green Hall
Grey Cot
Collpitts Esqr
Killingworth
Monk Seaton
Whitley
Horton Esqr

Gosforth House
Brandling Esqr
SHIRE MOOR
Dillercoats
Shipley

Callerton
Newbiggin
Kenton
Coxlodge
Gosforth
Longbenton
Forest Hall Fenton Esqr
High Flatworth
Preston
Monk Stone
Tinmouth
Castle in Ruins

Ouse Burn
Longbenton
Willington
Willington
Chirton
NORTH SHIELDS
TYNE MOUTH

Wharton Moor
Bulby
TOWN MOOR The Race Ground
Jesmond
Busy Cottage
Jigger
Benton House
High Main
Hayden
Pans
SOUTH SHIELDS

Montague Main
Old Cot
Fenham
NEW CASTLE
Heaton Hall
Walker
Walls End
Dock
Smith

Bakers Main
Elswick
Byker St Anth
RIVER TYNE
Jarrow
Low Water
Westoe
North Point

Derwent Haugh
Scotswood
Redheugh
GATESHEAD
Gateshead Park
Felling Hall Brandling Esqr
Brandling Main
Hebron
Monkton
Hedworth
Harton
Cleadon
Brit Point
Marston Rock

Bladon Main
Swalwell
Dunston
Wardley
Crow Hall
West Boldon
East Boldon
Whitburn
Cleadon
Cape Carr
Steel Rock

Whickham
Sheriff Hill
Low Moor
White House Stafford Esqr
Hilton Castle
Fulwell
Sea Point
Hole Point

Fellside
Sunniside
Ravensworth Castle
Team
Avon Bank
Usworth Hall
Suddick
Monk Wearmouth
WEAR MOUTH

Marley Hill
Langesley
Black Fell
Birtley
Usworth Main or Russell's Main
Mount Moor
Washington
Bramston
High Ford
Patton Goodshill Esqr
Bishop Wearmouth
SUNDERLAND
Hendon Lodge
Hendon Bay

Tanfield
Beamish
Beamish South Moor
Orpeth
Pelton Moor
Lee Field
Harraton
Boundary Moor
North Biddick
Harrington's Main
Whetton
Otterton
RIVER WEAR

Preach's Main
Biddick
Harraton
Lambton Hall
Lambtons Main
Panshen
West Harrington
East Harrington
Silksworth
Tunstall
Ryhope
Ryhope Bay

Chester le Street
Corn Moor
Newbottle
Burn Moor
Newbottle
Primrose Moor
Houghton le Spring
Burdon
Seaton
Dean
Seaham
Ryhope Dean

Deanry Moor
CHESTER COMMON
Great Lumley
Morton Hall
Duck
Dalton
Ruins

Men hacked the coal from outcrops on the sides of valleys, following the seam in or getting at it by clearing away the 'overburden' of other material until it became too thick for this to be possible. Some seams could also be reached by driving a tunnel upwards into them from the side of a valley; this had the advantage of being self-draining, since any water in the seam ran off down the tunnel – though, of course, there was no guarantee that some unlucky miners would not find themselves in the way of a torrent at the moment the seam was struck. A third method, used where coal seams were not too far beneath the surface (generally not more than 20 feet), was to sink a shaft and excavate the coal round it in a rough circle, until further work became unsafe;

---

1   *This plan of 1787 shows the collieries dotted along the rivers Tyne and Wear, the oldest great coal-mining district in Britain. Notice the waggonways leading from each pit to the river; for centuries coal was transported more efficiently by water than by land.*

2   *The collier as pictured in George Walker's book* The Costumes of Yorkshire *(1814). Behind him are an early locomotive and a pithead.*

---

then a new shaft was sunk a few yards away, and the procedure was repeated. For obvious reasons, these were known as 'bell' or 'beehive' pits.

Most of these methods were not very efficient. They were often just a profitable sideline for landowners, whose farm labourers were kept busy digging coal for them during off-seasons when there was no work to be done on the land. Until the late seventeenth century, only the North-East was a 'mining area', with ever-deeper shafts, a full-time workforce and a grim industrial landscape as evidence of the intense activity taking place. But gradually other areas – the Midlands, Yorkshire, Scotland, Cumbria, South Wales, Somerset – developed in the same direction.

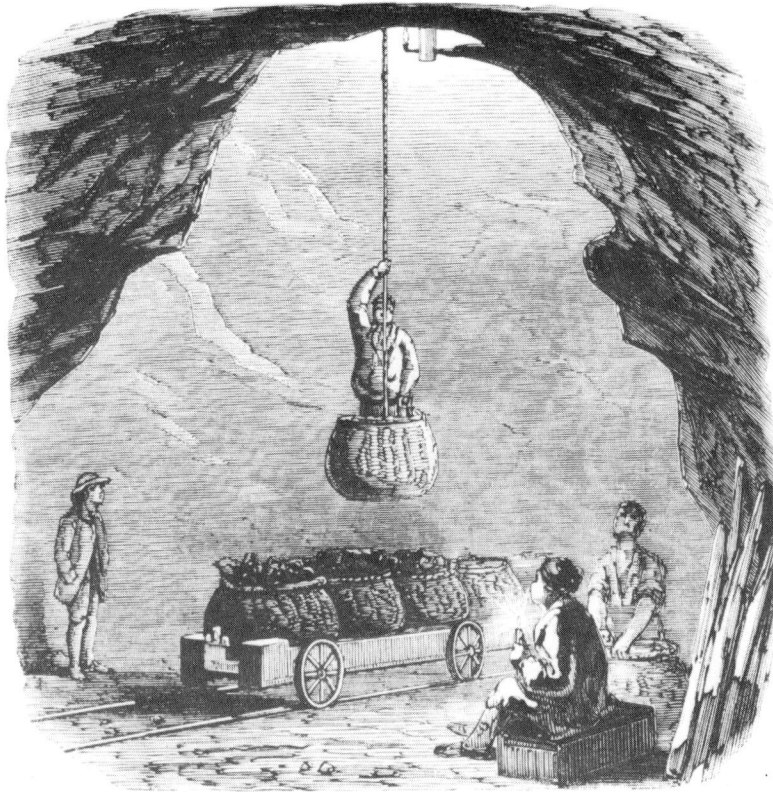

3 *Two hazards of early mining are obvious in this engraving: descending in an open basket and using naked lights that could easily cause an explosion on contact with gas.*

Miners seem to have been regarded from a very early date as a race apart. People evidently believed that only some kind of savage would go against nature as the miner did, living in dirt, foul air and darkness. They shunned him, and so he became clannish and rough, confirming the unfavourable ideas held about him. The status of the miner is shown by a judgment of 1699, in which 17 convicts had their sentences remitted in return for binding themselves to work in the mines for five years: mining was as bad as penal servitude. In Scotland it was literally serfdom: until as late as 1799, long after most other feudal practices had been abolished, the miner and his family remained tied to the laird's land, forbidden by law to move away or change his hereditary occupation. Often, as if to emphasize their degenerate nature, miners were even refused burial in consecrated ground.

Conditions of work were unpleasant and dangerous from first to last. Colliers were wound down the pit shafts sitting in the loops of ropes, and worked by the light of candles, despite the risk of an explosion if gas was present in any quantity. The risk was increased by the braziers placed at the bottom of the mine shaft to provide a certain amount of fresh air (warm air travels upwards, creating a current), and by the gunpowder used to break up the coal face. Safety precautions were almost non-existent, and as the mine workings became more extensive and deeper, the ways narrowed and became hotter, dustier and wetter. Men heaved and shovelled the coal, but much of the hauling was done by women and children, who could negotiate passages too low for the other beasts of burden, the pit ponies.

'King Coal'

From about 1760 onwards, Britain was transformed by the Industrial Revolution, and

4 *This mid-nineteenth-century illustration gives some idea of what unchecked industrialization did to the British landscape.*

became a land of teeming cities, busy factories, steam power and railways. By the middle of the nineteenth cenutry she was producing and exporting goods on a scale that had never been seen before. The proud subjects of Queen Victoria boasted that Britain was 'the Workshop of the World' and demonstrated the fact by holding the Great Exhibition of 1851 in London's Hyde Park.

There were plenty of ingenious machines and splendid artifacts at the Exhibition, but the most prominent item put on display by the coal industry was a gigantic lump of coal, symbolically placed close to the entrance. For coal, still won from the earth by sheer muscle-power, was indispensable to the entire industrial system: it smelted iron, powered factory machinery, drove the locomotives and steamships, and kept warm the rapidly multiplying population.

The accelerating demand for coal hardly benefited the miners themselves; in many cases they were probably even worse off than before. Deeper mines meant harsher conditions and greater risks – all the more so since few owners made proper maps of their often maze-like workings, in which children could get lost and trapped men might prove difficult to locate.

Even more important was the fact that early nineteenth-century employers tended to be pitiless taskmasters, encouraged by the prevailing economic philosophy of *laissez-faire*.

5 *Work going on in a Staffordshire mine. This is a 'pillar and stall' mine, in which the colliers left uncut pillars of coal to support the roof.*

This can be roughly translated as 'don't interfere' or 'let things alone'. It was based on the belief that if every man was left alone to work for his own advantage, without rules or restrictions, the resulting competition and conflict would benefit everybody by bringing about a highly productive and efficient society. In practice, employers and workers did not operate on equal terms, and wages and conditions in the new industrial Britain were appalling. Colliers were often exploited through protracted (12-year!) apprenticeship bonds and other legally enforceable agreements. The worst pits were those in the Midlands run on the 'butty' system, in which the butty or charter master acted as a middleman between owners and colliers; he contracted to produce a fixed quantity of coal for the owners, and slave-drove his workforce to meet his targets. Whether working for a butty or for piece-rates (i.e. by the amount of coal he produced rather than the number of hours he worked), the collier had little incentive to develop finer feelings or safety consciousness. It was he who paid the women and children who hauled the coal he had won, and he usually drove them on brutally with blows and curses. He also grudged the unpaid time needed to take safety precautions, and he was inclined to cut corners – literally. The method of working in many of the larger mines was 'pillar and stall', which involved tunnelling into the coal seam, leaving uncut pillars of coal to support the roof; but, all too often, miners were tempted to 'rob the pillar', cutting away more and more of the easily accessible coal of the pillar until what remained was dangerously –

10

sometimes catastrophically – slender. On every level, relations between masters and men were touched with hostility and suspicion. When the employers weighed the coal a man had won and calculated his pay, the result often seemed suspiciously meagre to the collier; and in some places he was virtually forced to spend vouchers, cash or credit at a high-priced 'tommy shop' owned by relatives or associates of the employer.

Reform

This 'truck' system disappeared in the 1840s, which also witnessed the first attempts to improve conditions down the mines by legislation.

6   *Child mine-workers in the 1840s. Until the Act of 1842, far younger children than these were often employed underground.*

7   *Women coal-bearers. In this picture they look quite sprightly, but a little imagination will suggest the likely effects of carrying dead weights up a steep incline all day.*

Humanitarians had already begun to agitate against bad conditions in factories, but the turn of the mines – less accessible and hidden from daylight observation – came only after an investigation by parliamentary Commissioners in the 1830s. They were appointed to find out how terrible disasters such as the Wallsend colliery explosion (in which 102 people were killed) could occur, and their report found:

That there are many mines in which the most ordinary precautions to guard against accidents are neglected, and in which no money appears to be expended with a view to secure the safety, much less the comfort, of the workpeople.

They also reported:

That partly by the severity of the labour and the long hours of work, and partly through the unhealthy state of the place of work, this employment . . . deteriorates the physical constitution.

And in the lowest working areas, where the coal seam was thin and men hewed coal in incredibly cramped conditions, 'the limbs become crippled and the body distorted'.

But what shocked the Commissioners most deeply was the treatment of women and children. According to the notions of the time, men were capable of looking after themselves, but it was accepted that 'the weaker sex' and small children, should be treated with kindness and consideration. Instead, the Commissioners found, 'instances occur in which children are taken into the mines to work as early as four years of age', usually for at least 11 hours a day. Many infants spent their time alone in the darkness, 'trapping' (opening and shutting ventilation doors for wagons to pass through), while others hauled tubs

---

8   *A woman 'drawer' was little more than a half-naked beast of burden. Sketches like this one were included in the report of the parliamentary Commissioners and shocked Parliament into passing the 1842 Act.*

9 *'Pit-brow women' at Rose Bridge Pits, 1865. The 1842 Act stopped women going underground, but at some places they continued to do heavy work at the pithead.*

of coal, going on all fours down the narrow tunnels. Women were similarly employed. One witness whom the Commissioners interviewed, Betty Harris, worked a 12-hour day down a pit at Little Bolton:

I have a belt round my waist, and a chain passing between my legs, and I go on my hands and feet . . . . The pit is wet where I work, and the water comes over our clog-tops always, and I have seen it up to my thighs . . . . My clothes are wet through almost all day long . . . . I have drawn till I have had the skin off me; the belt and chain is worse when we are in the family way [pregnant].

The outcome of the Commissioners' Reports was the first legislation controlling conditions below the surface – the Mines Act of 1842, which prohibited the employment of women, girls, and boys under the age of ten.

During the rest of the nineteenth century, the miner's lot improved considerably. This was partly thanks to parliamentary legislation and partly to technological improvements and the continued expansion of the industry. The introduction of steam pumps had improved drainage, and from 1815 the use of the Davy safety lamp somewhat reduced the danger of explosions caused by contact between naked flames and pockets of gas. Mechanical ventilating fans were introduced in the 1860s, safety fuses and manufactured explosives replaced gunpowder, winding was mechanized, and by the early twentieth century electrically driven ropes were doing much of the hauling; coal-cutting machines and conveyor belts were nineteenth-century novelties which were not widely employed at once, but were obviously of great importance for the future.

The grosser forms of exploitation disappeared: 'truck' became illegal and the butties were gradually replaced by coal companies, which were better able to bear the heavy costs of deep mining. Colliers were allowed to employ their own checkweighman to ensure that they were paid properly. After the Hartley Pit disaster of 1862, in which 204 men suffocated, it was made

10 'The First Fireman' igniting a pocket of methane gas so that it will burn off before collecting in dangerous quantities

compulsory for collieries to have two shafts, so that if one was blocked there would still be a source of air and an escape route. A 'cage' or covered-in lift gradually began to be used for carrying men and materials up and down the shafts in relative safety. Other safety regulations were enforced as far as possible by government inspectors, but there were all too few of them, and mine-owners did everything they could to avoid the extra trouble and expense involved. As a result, some major disaster continued to occur every few years, taking hundreds of lives and reminding people that the miner's job was still a hazardous and harsh one.

Into the twentieth century

The breakneck growth of the coal industry reached its climax in the late nineteenth and early twentieth centuries. The national output, roughly 10 million tons in 1800, reached about 54 million tons by 1850 and then soared to 250 million tons in 1900. The number of people employed in coalmining reached, and then passed, the million mark. Mining villages dotted the coalfields of Britain, and collieries were established in an entirely new area – Kent. Trade unionism became a force, helping colliers to realize how much the economy depended on their labour. There were setbacks in bad times – in 1893 the miners were forced to accept a 25 per cent cut in wages after a 16-week strike – but, when the recession was over, with coal production still rising in line with demand, the twentieth-century outlook seemed bright for both miners and the mining industry.

2 Colliers At Work

During the first half of the twentieth century, hopes of progress in the coal industry were largely disappointed. Wages and conditions of work hardly improved and, at times, even deteriorated; demand for coal was patchy; and further mechanization of the industry was very slow and limited in scope. The general history of the industry is traced in Chapters 1 and 3. This chapter describes the working lives of the colliers – and, just because changes occurred so slowly, the picture drawn is broadly true of conditions over a very long period, from the later nineteenth century to the 1940s and beyond.

A basic guide to the pit

Approaching a colliery, a visitor would see the pithead – a cluster of buildings, plant and machinery on the surface, dominated by the great, wheel-like winding sheaves; round these passed the winding ropes that lowered and raised men, equipment and huge quantities of coal. Everything that went into the pit, or came out of it, was carried in 'cages' suspended from the winding ropes. The cages were basically large lifts; each of the two vertical shafts contained two cages, one automatically rising as the other went down.

The area around the base of the shaft is known as the 'pit bottom'. From there a main 'road' or 'gate' – the commonest names for all tunnels underground – ran towards the workings, with various lesser roads branching off and terminating at a particular face. The coal face is the wall of coal that confronts the face-workers –

the men who actually shift the coal from the face, whether they use picks, explosives or coal-cutting machines. By the twentieth century the main method of coal-getting was not pillar-and-stall (described in the previous chapter), but 'longwall', which involved removing the entire seam. The face-workers advanced steadily, propping the newly exposed roof as they went on, and shovelling the coal they had won into 'tubs' or on to conveyor belts for pit ponies or engine-driven ropes to haul to the pit bottom. The coal, like the men, went to the surface in the cage.

Starting at a colliery

Coalmining tended to be a family occupation, if only because there were few opportunities to do anything else in a mining village. Jeffrey Jennings, a collier's son, started work at Shipley in 1931:

I left school at fourteen and I was about fourteen and a half then. Jobs were very scarce in those days, same as they are today. I had a good paper round, and my father said: 'Well – hang on to your paper round and don't go down the pit. Find a job somewhere else.'

But Jeffrey Jennings ended up at the colliery all the same. Like many others, he was put 'on the screens' to start with, picking out slag from the coal which had just been brought up from the pit. The screening plant was essentially a conveyor belt which was fed with coal by a tippler or dumper; this device emptied the contents of one tub after another on to a steel chute which conveyed them down to the belt. The noise it made was deafening, the atmosphere was dusty and often stifling, and the work was monotonous and hard on the back. Nevertheless, this was boys' work (or, in some places, women's work) and therefore, badly paid. Understandably, many boys could hardly wait to go underground, where the money was better and only worked on the screens until they reached the age at which this was legally allowed. Bernard Taylor became a screen worker in 1908, when he was 13, earning 1s. 3d. a day; when he was 14 the law allowed him to work underground at Sherwood Colliery, Mansfield Woodhouse, on 2s. a day – a 60 per cent increase.

Going down

At the pithead, the underground worker was issued with a lamp, which had to be checked before he went down by an official called a 'deputy'. He also received a tag with his number on, since it was important to know exactly who was underground if there was a serious accident such as an explosion. Then:

You go down the pit in a cage. There are usually three decks in a cage. The two lower decks are only the height of a tub, and so in those you had to crouch – all the men crouched on their hunkers [haunches]. On the top one of the three decks you had room to stand up. They drop you down, and halfway down the shaft you hear the other cage going back up, and yours slows down.

That was what it was like for Frank Crosland, who spent two years during the Second World War at the Maude Pit, Backworth, between Newcastle and Whitley Bay. Then – as now – the cage travelled faster than an ordinary lift, in most cases descending several thousand feet in a few

11 *Clay Cross No.2 Pit, 1910.*

CLAY CROSS NO. 2 PIT — 1910
MEMORIES ARE MADE OF THIS
GREETINGS FROM W. E. A.

minutes. 'It's a horrible sensation at first, but after that you take it for granted,' according to Frank Crosland. Most other colliers probably got used to it, although another wartime recruit, David Day, in his book, *The Bevin Boy*, remembers:

The first seconds are the worst with your stomach gyrating and the wind roaring up your trouser legs as the cage hurtles downwards. By the time you have reached the bottom your eardrums seem to have caved in, but this feeling is remedied by pinching your nose and blowing hard . . . . I don't think I ever got used to this early morning drop. I used to think of it as the black minute when everything became dark and noisy as the cage roared downwards, and my fear of the rope breaking never quite went until the lights of the pit bottom had come into view.

As we shall see, accidents were frequent enough in the industry to justify such fears. Even in our

12 *Pit bottom – the area around the mine shaft: a relatively pleasant place, with electric lighting and wide, well-supported tunnels*

more safety-conscious times something can go wrong with the cage – and in fact did so at Markham Main Colliery in 1973, where 13 men were killed.

Walking out

To newcomers who expected darkness and dirt, the pit bottom came as a pleasant surprise. Frank Crosland:

When you get to the bottom of a mine it's open; there are electric lights, and there's a certain amount of space to walk about in. It's all busy with the lines of tubs coming and going from the foot of the shaft. It's rather like a railway station junction.

You walked out from there. Sometimes you walked up a main road; sometimes you walked up a by-road, which was very dusty indeed. But the main road's fairly smooth. You walk along there, then after half a mile or so it becomes lower down; there's about four feet of room. You go nodding your head all the time; if your head goes too high you bump it – and you know about it.

Like most other miners, Frank Crosland made light of the physical discomforts that had to be endured. As Jeffrey Jennings put it:

I don't think comfort came into working at t'pit – you never bothered about comfort. It's because you go into it young – and you just accept it, don't you?

In reality, even walking out to the face could be very hard work. Though shafts were sunk close to the coal seam, the face constantly moved further away as more and more coal was removed. Men commonly walked a mile or two underground before starting their shift – and, of course, beginning to earn money. And in a few pits they might have to walk up to five miles. They also had to stoop most of the way while simultaneously keeping their heads cocked so they could check the roof for projecting lumps of rock or broken-down supports. And they had to do it all over again at the end of a shift lasting at least eight hours (until very recent times) and generally involving the hardest kind of physical labour.

The darkness of the pit

Off the main road, everything lay in a darkness broken only by the lamps the men carried. Here there was not the faintest trace of sun- or moonlight, and if your lamp went out it was quite impossible to see your own hand in front of your face. Ex-miners become particularly eloquent on this subject. In his autobiography, *My Generation*, the union leader Will Paynter recalls being left alone when the man he was working with was called away:

I accidentally caused my lamp to overturn and go out. I was 'in the dark' as they say in the pit. It is hard to describe this darkness of the pit. It is absolute blackness, impenetrable and eerie. Sounds appear to be magnified, the creaks of roof movement sounding like cracks of doom and the falling of loose pieces of coal from the front of the coal face becoming frightening crashes, noises that are normal to the pit, heard and ignored in the presence of some light and company. The man and boy in the next working place could not hear my shouts and the tears came as I had to crawl in darkness, feeling my way as best I could until they were able to hear me.

The 14-year-old Will Paynter cried in the darkness of a mine in South Wales, towards the end of the First World War. A few years earlier, in 1909, another 14-year-old, Bernard Taylor, went underground at Sherwood Colliery; and, like the even smaller and younger children of earlier times, he started as a trapper, opening the ventilation doors so that the ponies pulling the tubs of coal could pass through, and then making sure the doors were closed again. As it was a simple enough operation to fit automatically closing doors, the trapper's job had already become obsolete, and at Sherwood seems to have been continued as a kind of introduction to life underground, while you were 'getting your pit eyes'. In *Uphill All The Way*, Taylor – later a Member of Parliament and, from 1966, a Life Peer – writes:

The memory of sitting behind the door alone and most of the time in darkness still haunts me, in spite of the many years that have passed since 1909. You were isolated and the Davy Safety Lamp was easily extinguished; the door trapper's lamp had to be lent to the pony drivers, who were responsible for a constant supply of tubs to the men at the coal face . . . for most of the day this was happening; when one lamp had been relighted, another had gone out, and there you were alone, and afraid, in the darkness, listening to the timber roof supports cracking and making weird noises – and at fourteen years

13 *Hewing coal. In Britain, coal was 'hand got' in some places until quite recent times.*

of age the mind is impressionable. Pit darkness has to be experienced to be believed.

At the face

When a boy first went underground, he usually worked with the ponies, shovelled coal dust, or performed some similar task. In South Wales, however, boys like Will Paynter could go straight on to the face, where the most exhausting work of all was done. Paynter's job was to keep pushing large 'curling boxes' into place for the collier to fill with the coal he had won; both of them operated in a space 2ft 6in. high – the height of the seam – so that the collier worked on his side while the boy pushed in a near-horizontal position. Over the next few years he would pick up the colliers' skills by working alongside them; this was the closest thing to a training scheme in British mines before they were nationalized in 1947.

The coal face was usually several hundred yards long, and divided into 'stalls'. There might be one stall to a collier, or a number of colliers might share the same stall; since they tended to have large families, it was quite common for

14 *The holer at work. He hacked away a strip at the bottom of the coal face (wall) so that the rest would be easier to bring down; usually he went in so deep that he disappeared from sight.*

fathers and sons, or brothers, to work together. In some places a modified, less pernicious form of the butty system operated: such a 'little butty' was generally an experienced miner who contracted to get the coal from a particular stall and reckoned to make only a few shillings more than the daymen he had hired to work beside him.

Working under a low ceiling was not an occasional feature of existence on the face, but part of the everyday routine. There was never any question of cutting away tons of rock from the ceiling just to give the collier more space in which to wield his pick and shovel: he aimed to shift coal and nothing but coal, working at the height of the coal seam, whatever that might happen to be. (In practice, of course, a certain amount of rock came down with the coal, but to the collier that was an annoyance, not an advantage.) In some places the seam might be as little as 18in. high; 3ft 6in. was considered a good height to work in, and relatively few seams went very much higher.

If the coal seam was close to the surface, it might be relatively cool at the face. In most of the larger, deeper mines, it was very hot. Colliers stripped off as they made their way 'inbye' to the face, and worked in nothing but helmet, underpants, knee-pads, and clogs or boots; in some places the heat was so intense that they worked stark naked. The colliers, working individually or in small groups in separate stalls, were isolated by the darkness as they 'got' the

coal by the dim light of their lamps. These men working at the face with picks and shovels were what most people think of when they hear the word 'miners'. They were the heroes of the colliers' own stories and legends – the 'Big Hewers' who could shift coal as if they were power-driven, using mighty muscles that never tired. The introduction of real machines was to change all this, but only very slowly.

Where the coal was entirely 'hand got', the first operation was carried out by the 'holer', who used his pick to remove a strip of coal a few inches high from the bottom of the face. He worked on his side, entirely disappearing from view, until he had reached the furthest point (probably about 5ft deep) from which coal would be removed during that shift. When the holer had finished and wriggled out, most of the props he had put under the coal were knocked away. The weight of the roof above the undercut area weakened the coal, or even caused it to collapse. If the coal was hard, explosives were generally used to weaken it further, though the more primitive pits, such as the one at which Bill Haywood started work in 1910, still relied on sheer manpower:

15 *A model of a 1929 coalcutter, which took over the job of holing. It reduced the physical labour involved in mining, but created a fearful noise and poisonous quantities of dust.*

We didn't use a lot of powder in those days: only to move stone. You got your coal with a pick – a pick and shovel. The machines took a lot of the hard work out.

Although introduced before the end of the nineteenth century, coal-cutting machines were adopted only very gradually; even in 1925, just one colliery in five – generally the bigger and more modern ones – had cutters. But the change, though slow, was inexorable, and by 1947 the amount of coal still 'hand-got' was down to 20 per cent. As so often in the history of the coal industry, 'progress' had its drawbacks, as Frank Crossland explains:

This enormous thing weighs about three tons. It's very solid – everything's very solidly made down the pit – and armour-plated. It has a long arm, rather like a chain saw, but much heavier of course, with picks that rotate. It makes a tremendous noise, and it draws itself along on a steel chain which is anchored to a sloping post.

Two men operate it, one going in front, the other following behind clearing any debris and making sure the machine's going all right. It's a rather dangerous thing because it's so noisy that if a fall of stone were to start you wouldn't hear any warning sounds. It's very, very dusty – you can hardly see the end of your shovel in front of you, and it's not a pleasant thing to be with.

The writer George Orwell was more emphatic in his book *The Road to Wigan Pier:*

Incidentally it makes one of the most awful noises I have ever heard, and sends forth clouds of coal dust which make it impossible to see more than two or three feet and almost impossible to breathe.

21

16 *Using the coal-burster. This is a hydraulic cartridge which is fitted against a shot-hole; high pressure water and oil are pumped through it to break down the coal – a safer alternative to explosives.*

After the undercutting, if the coal was 'easy getting' the collier pulled it down with his pick. If it was 'difficult getting' the shot-firer came and drilled holes in the face, packed them with explosives – slow explosives, so that the subsequent blast would not shatter the coal into tiny fragments.

What was 'easy getting' like? Norman Harrison, who worked at Snowdown Halt, Kent, in the 1940s, gives an ironic answer in *Once a Miner:*

Coal is easy stuff to get. You bang it with the pick head and where it sounds good you throw the slim, dagger-like blade in and lever . . . .
Yes, coal is easy stuff to get, but after half a shift of hewing and shovelling it you sometimes wonder what you've been doing all the time. Even when the coal is like a sack of flour, pouring out, even then it seems incredible that all you've sent away down the [conveyor] belt only amounts to so much, say four or five tons.

The understatement in this becomes easier to appreciate after reading Orwell, who estimated that, as a keen gardener, he could shift two tons of earth in an afternoon – but earth, not coal, and not working on his knees or after walking miles underground.

Even when explosives brought down all the coal and made the face worker just a 'filler', he remained an object of admiration to men such as Frank Crosland:

That's all they did, shovel it away on to the conveyor belt, which was behind them. Shovelling on their knees, behind them. Muscular men!

And Norman Harrison, describing his early struggles to keep up, writes:

For unremitting work I have never seen any surface worker of any calling who can compare with the collier. There are no stops for a cigarette, no stops for tea, no stops to pass the time of day with your neighbour. Even when the deputy [official inspector] passes he'll not stop unless he has something to say to you in particular. When a collier is trying he stops for snap exactly

A pit horse with the haulier and his assistant in 1910.
Photo: W.E. Jones

twenty minutes . . . and six to eight times to drink, each time being perhaps a minute by the watch. (*Once a Miner*)

The collier drank, easing his dusty throat, from a bottle which, in the hotter mines, might contain up to eight pints of water or cold tea. 'Snap' was his bite to eat, usually a few slices of bread and jam or dripping. He carried it in a 'snap tin' which more or less kept out the dust and protected it from the attentions of mice, who had somehow established themselves and managed to survive in most pits. 'I soon got into the habit of working in that unremitting way,' writes Norman Harrison. 'To get my coal off I had to.'

17   *A pit horse with the haulier and his assistant, 1910. Pit ponies spent their entire lives underground and developed a legendary sense of danger which saved many human lives.*

Ponies, conveyors and ropes

When the coal had been shovelled into waggons ('tubs') at the face, it was transported to the pit bottom and taken to the surface in the cage. For a long time the hauling underground was done by pit ponies, and a large colliery might keep several hundred of them. Normally their drivers were boys – like Bill Haywood, whose memory goes back to the years before the First World War:

I used to gang wi' ponies, you know – they pulled waggons. There used to be close on a hundred ponies at that pit at one time. Well looked-after? I wouldn't say that; but they kept them going. I've seen them with sores on their shoulders, where they've caught the rope. All under the collar, raw with pulling. Terrible time for ponies, in my opinion.

Jeffrey Jennings found much the same conditions in the 1930s ('Like skeletons, some of 'em'), although some ponies were very well cared for and developed a loving relationship with their drivers. In most places there seems to have been little deliberate cruelty but a good deal of callousness: in the hard-driven underground world of the coal mines, a pony received short shrift if it could not, or would not, drag heavy loads; and whereas the men and boys worked shifts, all too often the same ponies were used from one shift to the next. Perhaps the most extraordinary thing – to us – is that pit ponies spent their entire lives underground; the only times they saw daylight were during the long national strikes of 1921 and 1926, when they were brought to the surface and allowed to graze in fields.

When old miners reminisce, they almost always mention the 'cleverness' of the ponies, and the number of lives they saved. The colliers themselves had a well-developed sense of danger, reacting instantly to the creaking of timbers, the sensation of a few grains of rock dropping on the neck, and other early warnings of a roof fall or some other mishap. But the pony's instincts were keener still, and in similar cases it would shy, or refuse to budge, long before the humans realized anything was wrong. And every novice down the pit would be told that, if he became lost in the dark, he should hold on to the tail of a pony, which would infallibly bring him back to the pit bottom.

Eventually conveyor belts replaced pit ponies, though the process was a very slow one, since the belts were not easily adapted to the rugged, irregular conditions underground. Three roads

18 An 'onsetter' at work in 1926, pushing tubs into the cage (lift). Given the pressure under which men worked underground, this job required great strength and very quick reactions.

led to the coal face – a relatively spacious central road and two smaller side roads whose main purpose was to enable air to circulate. Typically, the conveyor belts ran from each end of the face, all along it and for some distance down the central road, which was also the main route for supplies going up to the face. Like the coal-cutting machines, they made a 'frightful, deafening din' and the men worked in a 'fog of dust' (George Orwell, The Road to Wigan Pier). At the far ('outbye') end, the belt was raised several feet high, so that the coal poured down endlessly into the tubs, which were shunted, one after another, under the belt and away again. Then the loaded tubs were lashed with chains to the power-driven steel rope that carried them to the pit bottom, where they were uncoupled and sent up to the surface in the cage; meanwhile a second steel rope carried empty tubs to be uncoupled and loaded.

This sounds a simple enough series of operations, but, in practice, the sheer pace of work called for strength, skill and quick reactions on the part of the men involved in loading and haulage. The conveyor went on relentlessly, never stopping unless there was a serious hold-up or accident. The four or five men working at the loading point had to shunt the tubs in and out of place, and push ('tram') them, when full, along the rails, often on a gradient – and had to do it continuously, for hours on end. Lashing the tubs on to the steel rope required skill, for the lashing was done while the rope was moving (it, too, never normally stopped), and nasty little accidents were common. Derailments, which held up work – and therefore earnings – had to be dealt with promptly. Frank Crosland:

When tubs came off the rails weighing nearly half a ton, some of these chaps could get their backs against them and heave, lifting or rocking them back into place.

But when David Day tried to do it, the result was disastrous. Although not a miner by choice (he was a wartime conscript), he became an efficient collier; and later he became an able writer. Yet he found haulage work beyond him:

The truth was that I was not cut out to be a haulage hand. I didn't have the quickness of mind or adroitness of hand essential for the job. I had realised this . . . when we were first taught how to clip and unclip tubs to a moving rope, and it had always been a relief to me that I had never been directed to haulage work. On this particular day however I had no alternative . . .
(*The Bevin Boy*)

All went well until one of a line of empty tubs appeared with its rear wheels off the rails. Trying to lift the moving tub back on, Day only succeeded in derailing it completely. Further efforts led to more derailments, and the situation became nightmarish as one calamity led to another. Trying to reach the bell wire to ring for the rope to stop, Day dropped his lamp. The empty tubs engaged with a line of loaded tubs going in the other direction, and in the darkness there was a terrible sound of crashing and tearing. When light was restored, Day found that some of the loaded tubs had been overturned, and another one had crashed into a roof girder, smashing it and bringing down quantities of timber and roof. To make good the damage

caused by this one-man catastrophe, the entire shift was held up for nearly an hour.

So much for simple operations underground.

Advancing the face

As the coal was cut away from the seam, the face advanced a few feet every day. Once a degree of mechanization had been achieved, the conveyor belts had to be dismantled and brought up to the new face. The old three-shift system, with hewers working round the clock, was modified so that the necessary procedures – machine-cutting and blasting, moving up the equipment and reinforcing the roof supports, and shifting the coal – were done in separate shifts.

As the face advanced, an empty 'waste' was created behind it. If supported and maintained, it would eventually have become an enormous underground gallery. But it was not (and, in modern mining practice, still is not) supported and maintained. The roof was allowed to collapse – in its own good time, as Frank Crosland recalls:

And then, a rather curious thing they do is to withdraw the supports behind, and then all the rock falls down. I remember we went in this place, it must have had a strong gritstone ceiling, and we must have been in for a week or ten days without anything happening. Then one night the thing started to go like an earthquake, and my friend said to me 'Get in the nook!' [a cubby-hole in the wall]. Great slabs came sliding down, and there were great blasts of air as they fell. It was a terrifying experience.

Although the waste behind the working area was allowed to collapse, the three roads leading to the face had to be maintained. They also had to be advanced, to keep up with the forward march of the face itself. This was another dangerous and difficult job, known as 'ripping'. The roads were advanced through the waste and, in the case of the more spacious central road, this meant that new rock had to be brought down to make a higher roof than the one at seam-height which the face workers had left; if the seam was 4ft high, for

19 *The nerve-racking side of mining: clearing debris after a roof fall*

example, the rippers would have to blast away another 8ft of solid rock to make a supply road 12ft high. Since the behaviour of a roof was unpredictable at the best of times, this was a nerve-racking operation; and it was even more nerve-racking when the rippers mounted movable scaffolds and began pulling down loose rock from the roof, remaining constantly on the alert in case more started to fall than they had bargained for. Then they would put up a series of large arched girders to support the roof, lining the spaces between with wooden boards. The fallen rock would be built up against the sides of the road as drystone walls ('packs'), giving the new roof extra support.

Craftsmen and managers

There were plenty of other arduous jobs to be done from time to time, including some that involved passing through places so low that even crawling was impossible. You could only wriggle – perhaps in search of a coal seam that had disappeared because of a geological fault, or to investigate the possibility of salvaging materials in exhausted workings.

A range of professional and craft skills was also needed, both below ground and on the surface, to make the pit work. Frank Crosland:

Other crafts? Well, there were surveyors, of course. And electricians and engineers and bricklayers. And blacksmiths – they were generally on the top. They were needed for all sorts of jobs. You see, the industry was still at that stage of technology when many things were fabricated on the spot. Everything was very simple and crude, so parts for the tub would be made on the pit bank. Or you could get your drill sharpened there, or your pony shod. So there was quite a big blacksmith's shop.

Like the colliers, the craftsmen were not trained by the mining company. Jeffrey Jennings was a 15-year-old surface worker when:

... the boss picked me out and asked me if I'd like to work on the electrical side. I had to go to mining school – but you had to go in your own time. You still had to do your six days' work. If I was on afternoons I'd go in the morning; if I was on days or nights I'd go in the evening.

The same was true of careers in management. Colliers could 'get on', but only if they had exceptional stamina as well as the necessary ability. One such was Jim Bullock, whose book *Them and Us* describes how he made his way up to colliery manager by passing examinations. To do so, he studied four nights a week at Technical School for six years, took correspondence courses and received private tuition – during all of which time he worked a six-day week to support his family.

The existence of an examination system represented a step forward, since it meant that the mines were run by men of reasonable technical competence – which had often been far from the case during the nineteenth century. Overall control lay with the colliery manager, who in technical matters worked in close consultation with the surveyor. Underground, the under-manager was in charge, assisted in most pits of any size by overmen who were responsible for groups of districts. At the bottom of the hierarchy, and most closely in touch with the colliers, came the deputy, who was himself normally an ex-collier.

The deputy was in charge of a district, an area underground of which he was supposed to make a complete tour twice in every shift: this was a government regulation, the deputy was primarily a safety officer, charged with issuing and checking the colliers' lamps, measuring the air pressure, testing for the presence of gas, and reporting on all aspects of safety. He alone acted as the shot-firer below ground, placing and detonating all explosives. And since it was important that he should be prepared to stop all work in his district if any danger threatened, he was paid a salary that remained unaffected by changes in productivity.

However, when Jim Bullock became a deputy:

The manager then gave me a lot of useful advice telling me that I now belonged to *them* and that I had to have the interests of the company at heart at all times. (*Them and Us*)

And in practice the deputy usually *was* a company man, acting as a roving foreman. In this, as in many other respects, the reality of twentieth-century coalmining was very different from the legal and theoretical situation.

Safety and sanitation

Operations underground were controlled by detailed regulations based on Acts of Parliament. But all too often the law was ignored or evaded. The owners did everything they could to avoid spending money, while the colliers understandably skimped on any activity that interfered with the work they were paid to do. Some colliers were also influenced by notions of 'manliness' or simple conservatism; for example, in the 1940s there were still face-workers who refused to wear safety helmets. Even the Davy lamp was only grudgingly accepted, though it was widely used since: even the least safety-conscious men realized that a naked flame could easily blow hundreds of people to kingdom come. The gauze surround of the lamp absorbed the heat of the flame, so that – unlike a naked light – it would not ignite a combustible mixture of gas and air. It was not, in fact, reliable in extreme conditions, but from the collier's point of view it had more serious everyday disadvantages: it easily went out if knocked over, and above all, it gave a very dim light – about one-eighth the strength of an average candle – which was unpleasant to work by and tended to bring on eye troubles. As a result, there were still some pits where insane risks were taken. As late as 1910, when Bill Haywood started work:

They'd all got matches in that pit, then; wouldn't believe that, would you? Candles ... and us lads

had a little lamp wi' paraffin in: a little box lamp.
Why, one time there was a very strong wind in
the downcast shaft, and it blew out the under-
manager's lamp. He asked a chap – and this was
a chap who always carried a big hurricane
lamp:
  'Have you got any matches?'
  'I've got to have 'em, haven't I?' said the chap.
And he opened the under-manager's safety
lamp [which was supposed to be kept locked]
and lit it for him.

By the 1940s this problem, at least, had been
solved by the introduction of the cap lamp, which
was run off electric batteries.
  There were many less obviously dangerous
infringements: 'dust is loaded into any old tub,
haulage precautions are disregarded, ventilation
doors are propped open' (Norman Harrison,
writing of the 1940s in *Once a Miner*). Deputies
were often allocated larger districts than they
could effectively patrol, and deceiving
government inspectors seems to have been
regarded as standard practice. This was a
grotesque situation in occupations that were
bound to involve considerable danger even in
favourable circumstances. Immense pressures

buckled the best-supported roofs or pushed up
the floors. Jeffery Jennings:

That roof is alive, isn't it? Either the floor or the
roof; they're moving all the while. When the
coal's come away, naturally the rocks want to
come together . . . . I've seen no end of people
have a stone come down on 'em and break a leg
or something like that.

In addition to natural hazards such as gas and
falling rock, the sheer pace of the work, poor
lighting, bad maintenance, inadequate
inspection and sheer carelessness made
coalmining the most dangerous of all British
industries. Cuts, bumps and bruises went with the
job, and were not worth talking about; you could
usually identify a man as a miner from the blue
scars on his face or body, caused by coal (which
is aseptic) working its way into lacerations. Every
few years a disaster made newspaper headlines,
but injuries and deaths in any year reached
incredible heights. In the worst year – 1910 – 1818
men died, and in 1938 there were still 858
fatalities. It is harder to find reliable figures for
accidents (especially since most men worked on
in spite of them, if they possibly could), but it is
clear that they were everyday occurrences. If
you worked underground you expected to suffer
some kind of injury sooner or later, and your main

20 *A mine rescue brigade*

21 *Miners 'manriding' to the surface*

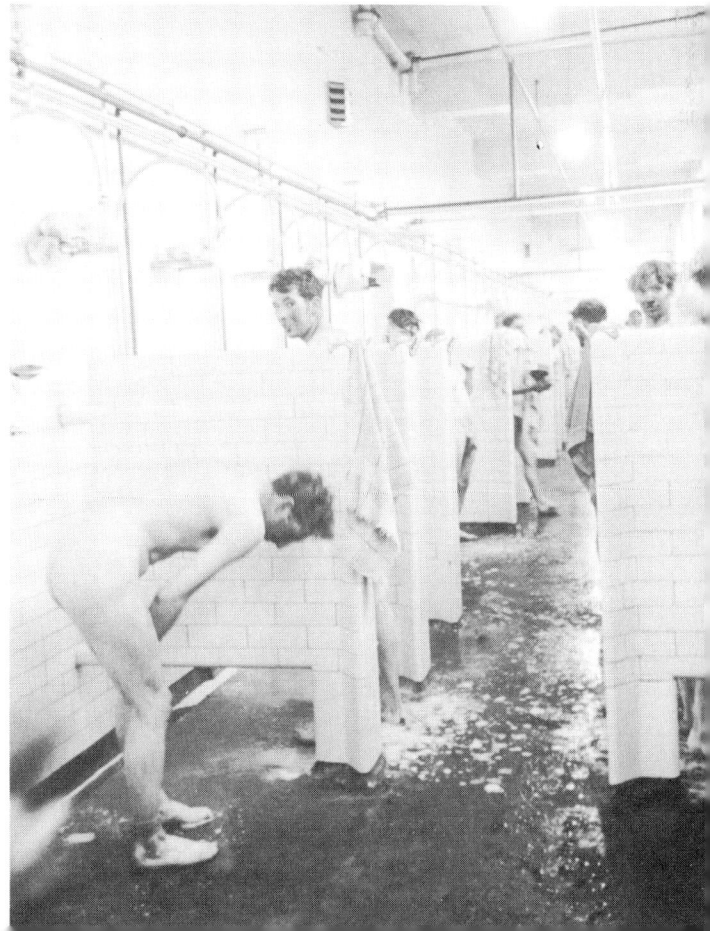

22 *Pithead baths made it possible for colliers to wash off their pit dirt before going home after work. This elementary amenity only became available to all miners after the Second World War.*

worry was how you would manage on the compensation paid by the colliery company. At 88, Bill Haywood remembered it all well:

My pal, brought up in a tub at Brinsley, with a broken back. They got £300 for three children. And Herbert Meakin: I remember I met them bringing his dad out dead. That's all *his* wife got – three hundred quid . . . . We had a train run away on us, 6 November, 1930, it was. Forty of us injured: I had a broken hand. And I had 25s. 4d. a week compensation, with a wife and two children to keep. Them – the good old days!

Finally, when a shift was over, most workers above and below ground were dirty. In fact, after cutters and conveyors had been installed, the face-worker was dirtier than he had ever been, his head and body plastered over with coal dust and sweat. Even on the surface, during the shift, Jeffrey Jennings found in 1931 that:

When you ate, you had dirty hands. There was nowhere to wash them: there was no water at all.

And the toilets were ridiculous – terrible – just a pan that was emptied occasionally. And you went home like that!

Yet some employers had installed pithead baths (actually showers) even before the First World War, and the government had wanted to make the provision of such 'baths' compulsory, until they were dissuaded by colliery owners who claimed that the men did not want them. Gradually baths were installed in some mines – usually bigger, more modern ones – between the World Wars; and perhaps one miner in three experienced the luxury of going home clean. Jeffrey Jennings:

I was lucky. They built a pithead bath about a year before the [Second World] War broke out [i.e. about 1938]. The colliery next to us got the foundations in but they didn't get theirs because of the War . . . . It were *beautiful*: super!

3 Hard Times: The Mines Before Nationalization

Before the First World War

The conditions described in Chapter 2 make it easy to understand why the earlier twentieth century was a period of bitter conflicts between mine-owners and mine-workers. The worst horrors of the Industrial Revolution had disappeared, but the work remained uniquely exhausting, dangerous, dirty and uncomfortable.

Writing in 1937, George Orwell thought that the pit was simply a vision of Hell:

23 *A commemorative photograph, created after the fire damp explosion on 20 February 1908 at the Glebe Colliery, County Durham, in which 14 men were killed*

DURHAM MINE DISASTER.
FIRE DAMP EXPLOSION AT THE GLEBE CO: RY.
WASHINGTON. Thursday February 20th 1908

14 MINERS CRUSHED & BURNT TO DEATH & ONE SERIOUSLY INJURED

DAMAGED UP-CAST SHAFT

GENERAL VIEW OF COLLIERY

STANLEY DISASTER
FUNERAL OF THE VICTIMS FEB. 21ST 1909. (B.

24 *Coalmining remained the most dangerous occupation in Britain. This funeral photograph was taken five days after the explosion at Stanley Pit, County Durham, on 16 February 1909, in which 168 lives were lost.*

25 *The agitation for an eight-hour shift, which finally succeeded when the Coal Mines Regulation Act of 1908 was passed*

Most of the things one imagines in hell are there – heat, noise, confusion, darkness, foul air, and, above all, unbearably cramped space. Everything except the fire, for there is no fire down there except the feeble beams of Davy lamps and electric torches which scarcely penetrate the clouds of coal dust. (*The Road to Wigan Pier*)

Some of this was unavoidable, but most perfectly feasible advances were fiercely resisted by the owners. They were often successful in drawing the teeth from Acts of Parliament, and either evaded or delayed putting into effect measures that might have improved the health, comfort or safety of the colliers. In the worst disaster in British coalmining history – the

26 *Miners voting in 1912 on whether or not to come out on strike. The action that ensued was the first national coal strike, involving over a million men.*

NOTICE!!!

The MINERS of the Dudley District are respectfully informed

THAT

A Public Meeting

Will be held at *The 5 Ways* on *Monday Oct. 7*

On business of importance to their welfare, and for the purpose of petitioning the next Sessions of Parliament to pass an **Eight Hours' Bill** for the Regulating and Working the Mines and Collieries of Great Britain.

The Meeting will be addressed by Mr. WM. DANIELLS, Editor of the *Miners' Advocate*, and one of the Agents of the MINERS' NATIONAL ASSOCIATION; also, by other friends of the Rights of Labour. Chair taken at *Three* **o'clock.**
Miners Attend, Remember "UNION IS STRENGTH."

(GOODWIN, PRINTER, NEW-ST., DUDLEY.)

INDUSTRIAL UNIONISM
AND THE
MINING INDUSTRY

BY GEORGE HARVEY.

Student at Ruskin College Oxford in 1908.

Editor of the Socialist 1911 - 1912.

Author of the First Pamphlet Published in Britain on this subject - in 1911 -

A Book for mineworkers by a lifelong mineworker.

PRICE, 1/-

Published by the Author at Miners Hall Wardley Colliery Pelaw on Tyne.

explosion in 1913 at the Universal Colliery, Sengenhydd, Glamorgan – 439 men died because legal safety requirements had been ignored; as in most cases of the sort, it was the manager who took the blame for carrying out the owners' policies.

However, in the early years of this century the miners made some important advances. The Coal Mines Regulation Act of 1908 limited to eight hours the shift a man could be required to work. After 1911 boys of 12 were no longer to be seen underground, though at 13 they could (and most did) take a job on the surface and go down a year later. And in 1912 the Minimum Wage Act finally gave some protection to the piece-worker whose stall happened to be underproductive through no fault of his own (for example, because the coal was especially hard, or twisted away through some quirk of geology). The piece-work system itself went on unaltered, requiring the company to issue elaborate printed lists of jobs and rates that were always a source of dispute and ill-feeling.

The 1912 Act was considered a landmark at the time. It was achieved after a long and bitter dispute, culminating in a six-week national strike – the first-ever national coal strike, involving over a million men. Strikers and police fought pitched battles and soldiers were drafted into militant areas such as the Rhondda and Aberdare Valleys in South Wales. Having long been entangled in a mass of local problems and local negotiations, the miners' unions gradually came together in a national organization – the Miners' Federation of Great Britain, and the success of the national strike held out the prospect of further gains to be won by united action.

For the miners were indispensable while Coal remained King. In 1913, the year before the First World War broke out, there were over 3000 coal mines, employing more than 1,100,000 men, and output climbed to a record figure of 287, 430, 473 tons. Coal was still the fuel that drove the Western world forward, and Britain was still able to export

it to eager foreign buyers. Occasional warnings of things to come – such as the changeover from coal to oil by the Royal Navy, which had begun in 1907 – went largely unnoticed.

In the event, 1913 proved to be the all-time peak year for the coal industry. Output was never again to be so large, and the hard times ahead were to show up the serious weaknesses of the industry: inefficient organization, obsolete working practices and equipment, the owners' unwillingness to change or invest money when and where it was needed – and, of course, bad relations between management and labour.

The Sankey Report (1919)

During the First World War, the government took over direction of the mines. This was done because coal was of vital importance to the war effort, and colliers were exempted from military service for the same reason. But such a temporary 'nationalization' also represented a striking vote of no confidence in the owners, and from a government that was certainly not friendly towards socialist ideas. This judgment was confirmed immediately after the War, when the government, threatened with a national strike, set up a Royal Commmission under Sir John Sankey to investigate the situation in the coal industry. The majority of the Commissioners favoured nationalization – not out of any direct sympathy for the miners, but because:

The relationship between the masters and workers of the coalfields in the United Kingdom is, unfortunately, of such a character that it seems impossible to better it under the present system of ownership.

In other words, relations between owners and miners were already so bad that there seemed no conceivable prospect of improving them. The experience of war had also given some of the Commissioners a new attitude towards vital national resources:

Coal is our principal national asset, and as it is a wasting asset, it is in the interests of the State

that it should be won and used to the best advantage.

The miners themselves wanted nationalization (the Federation had been affiliated to the Labour Party since 1909), but Sankey's solution was too radical for Lloyd George's conservative-oriented government. However, two other recommendations were accepted and implemented: a seven-hour shift was introduced, and wages were raised by two shillings a shift. At this point the miners

28 *The banner of a Durham miners' lodge, with 'Labour and Peace' as its motto. Like others of its kind, it conveys the generous hopes associated with the developing labour and socialist movements.*

were among the better-paid British workers. Most farm labourers, for example, received well under £2 a week in wages, and shop assistants not much more than £2. But, in South Wales, 16-year-old Will Paynter's wages went up to £3 as a result

of the Sankey Report, and a 22-year-old Nottinghamshire faceman on top rate, like Bill Haywood, took home £4. 4s. if he worked a full six shifts in a week. Only a few highly skilled working-class men – for example, railway engine drivers – could better this. For the moment, the miners, closely associated with the railwaymen and transport workers in 'the Triple Alliance', were a force to be reckoned with; and since the government was alarmed – rightly or wrongly – by the revolutionary sentiments sometimes heard in the disturbed post-war period, the awards to the miners may have been partly a way of buying them off or buying time. They were all the easier to afford because the end of the War brought an economic boom that lasted until the winter of 1920-1. Then it suddenly collapsed, and the bad times began.

The defeat of the miners

The 1920s and 1930s were decades of economic recession, although not all classes and occupations were equally affected and some

29 *Officials giving out miners' coal rations during the 1921 strike*

years were worse than others. During the worst period, between 1929 and 1932, the economy was in crisis and the number of people unemployed rose to well over three million. This was 'The Great Depression', a world-wide collapse that is recognized as a great historical disaster; but for many people in Britain, at least, the entire period between the World Wars was a difficult time. Britain's domination of international trade, already challenged, was ended by the First World War. Industries which had made her great, such as textiles and shipbuilding, began a decline that frantic reorganization seemed unable to check. And there were never, at any time between the Wars, fewer than a million people unemployed.

So the miners were not the only victims of the economic blizzard, though they were to become its most obvious casualties. General unemployment soared in the early months of

1921. In March, the government returned control of the coal industry to the owners, whose first action was to announce drastic wage-cuts commencing on 1 April. The miners rejected the cuts, and a national lock-out began. (A lock-out occurs when employers try to enforce a change in the terms of employment, refusing to take on any employee who wants to work on the old basis. By contrast, a strike occurs when the employees withdraw their labour in an attempt to exact new terms. Since strikes and lock-outs both involve employees deliberately staying away from work, the distinction is not always properly drawn, and the term 'strike' is often used to describe both situations.)

On 'Black Friday' – 15 April 1921 – the railwaymen and transport workers decided not to strike in sympathy with the miners, who were left to struggle on alone. On 1 July, after three months without work – and without pay – they were forced to capitulate and accept the lower wages offered.

Then, suddenly, the coal industry began to prosper again, though not because the owners' wage bills were lower. Britain's foreign competitors experienced difficulties that made it possible to export at a favourable price, and, for a time, it seemed that the worst was over. But, in 1925, cheaper German, Polish and American

30 *Miners digging for coal during the 1921 strike. This kind of digging was done outside the colliery, in places where the effort would not normally have been thought worth while (for example, in waste heaps); but during a strike it enabled miners to earn a little extra money.*

coal, extracted from larger, more highly mechanized pits, drove the British product out of the international market. With the majority of British collieries making a loss, the owners' response was to demand another severe cut in wages, to which they later added the demand that miners should again start working longer hours.

This produced a critical situation in which it seemed possible that all trade unionists would down tools in sympathy with the miners. To head off such a general strike, the government offered the industry a subsidy – eventually amounting to £23 million – to keep it going while another Royal Commission investigated. When the Samuel Commission reported in March 1926, it had nothing better to recommend than an immediate cut in wages combined with a measure of reorganization and improved working conditions at some time in the future. Since the owners refused to consider reorganization and the miners' slogan was 'Not a penny off the pay, not a minute on the day', there was little room for compromise. On 1 May 1926 the owners posted their new terms, and a second national lock-out began.

The year 1926 has become famous as the year of the General Strike. On 3 May the General Council of the TUC (Trade Union Congress) called out workers in many major industries in support of the miners; nine days later, on 12 May, they called off the General Strike without securing any meaningful solution to the dispute. This was an important event in trade union history, and its whys and wherefores have been debated at length ever since. But they are beyond the scope of this book – and, in any case, the General Strike was only a brief episode in the miners' struggle. They carried on alone into the summer of 1926. Bill Haywood recalls:

Everybody enjoyed themselves then. Lovely summers: two lovely summers we had, '21 and '26. If money'd been all right we'd not've wanted to go back. But we'd no money. I don't know how we carried on. Soup kitchens out in the street, on trestles. We went and sunk pits and got our own coal – some pits thirty feet deep. Lorries used to come from Nottingham and give us two pound a ton. When you could get a ton . . . . We trickled back in '26, same as they done [in the 1984-85 strike, which had just finished at the time of this interview]. We had about four bob [shillings] a day less than when we came out.

It was a bitter conflict. The novelist and poet D.H. Lawrence, a collier's son, returned to his home town, Eastwood in Nottinghamshire, and was startled by the change of atmosphere. He recorded his impressions in an essay, 'Return to Bestwood' (1926): 'In house after house, the families are now living on bread and margarine and potatoes.' Colliers got up before dawn and scoured the countryside desperately for blackberries to sell at fourpence a pound. 'It is another world. There are policemen everywhere, great big strange policemen . . . . And they exist, along the country-side, in thousands'. These 'blue-bottles' were not locals but strangers, brought in from outside, to protect

31 *South Shields miners during the 1926 strike*

the 'dirty ones', or blacklegs, who worked while others held out. Respectable colliers' wives now sometimes jeered at the police, Lawrence noticed, while strikers and blacklegs were coldly hostile, each ignoring the others' existence.

After six months of near-starvation, the miners went back to the pits on the owners' terms. They took a cut in wages and had to work longer hours when the government suspended its seven-hour-shift legislation. They were also forced to go back to negotiating district rates, a move which favoured the owners since it meant piecemeal, confusing local negotiations that could not easily be generalized into national disputes. There was widespread victimization of union activists, many of whom were blacklisted for years; Bernard Taylor, for example, could not get a job down the pit until August 1937. The Miners' Federation itself, weakened by defeat, and by the existence of a breakaway union favoured by the employers, was able to offer little resistance until the mid-1930s. And with the Depression came soaring unemployment.

Between 1926 and 1935 the employers had things their own way on the coalfields – but at a price. Miners who were desperate for work had to take whatever terms the owners offered; but jobs were scarce because the industry was in a bad way. Despite government encouragement, there was no significant reorganization, and modernization always lagged behind what was being done abroad. Wage-cuts failed to make British coal more competitive, the industry remained in the doldrums, and, for a time, some 40 per cent of the workforce was jobless. By the 1930s the face-worker, once among the 'aristocrats of labour', was the worst-paid of all skilled men, lucky to earn £3 in a week; even the skilled woman – the certificated shorthand typist – was better off, despite the fact that all British women were outrageously underpaid as a matter of course. The average skilled man earned £4 a week – 25 per cent more than the collier – and railway drivers earned a princely £5. 10s.! Other mine-workers were paid even less than face-workers; and there was the ever-present possibility of being laid off (made unemployed for a longer or shorter period) or put on short-time

working. Jeffrey Jennings recalls:

They used to put up a notice: No Work This Week . . . . Well, two pound would make a week's wage in those days, in the '30s. In fact I could work six days and perhaps only get about £2. I got about seven bob a shift, I think. When I was 21 I used to pay my mother 21 shillings board. And probably only got twice that, all told.

In fact I never got married until I was twenty-six, because we'd got no blinkin' money. You were *poor*. You'd perhaps go to a film on Saturday night, and go to a chip shop, and that'd be it! That was it for the week!

It was terrible in those days.

In the later 1930s, life improved a little for miners. In 1935 they won a small increase in wages (up to a shilling a day) after threatening to strike, and the split between the Miners' Federation and the breakaway Spencer Union was healed. Then the Second World War brought full employment and a heavy demand for coal to fuel the war effort. The government again took over direction of the industry, though day-to-day control remained with the peacetime managers. Twenty thousand young men were drafted into the pits to provide extra labour; these 'Bevin boys' (named after the Minister of Labour, Ernest Bevin) were chosen by lot from the men who would otherwise have been conscripted into the armed forces. The scheme was not very successful, and in other respects mines and miners performed poorly throughout the war. Antiquated workings, under-equipment and bad relations between management and men were not so easily overcome. Many people came to agree with Sankey that a completely fresh start – nationalization – was the only answer; and when a Labour government was returned to power in 1945, it became a certainty.

---

32 *1934: unemployed miners at Pontypridd; they are creating allotments on the rocky hillside above the Rhondda Valley in Wales. This was not done to kill time, but to help their families survive during the harsh years between the World Wars.*

4 A Way of Life

The pit village

More than most other people, miners have found their way of life shaped by the nature of their job. They have generally lived in communities so dominated by the industry that they are known as mining villages; and the underground workers, at least, have worked exclusively in contact with their own kind.

33 *A depressing picture of miners' houses and the general environment at Byers Green Colliery. This is a mining village and nothing else. The 'hill' behind the houses is in fact a waste-tip. The mine-shaft is just outside the picture, about a hundred yards to the left.*

34 *A typical Welsh mining village and colliery*

Mining communities developed because collieries had to be set up where the coal seams lay and miners had to live close to the collieries. Some of these were near enough to large towns to share in their way of life, but most were sprinkled over the British coalfields, relatively isolated even from one another. This was not necessarily a matter of great distances: until the motor car became a common working-class possession, even a few miles was enough to make a 'trip into town' a fairly infrequent event. As a result, miners remained strongly regional in outlook and speech, and used a great variety of local terms in their work, so that groups of men from different regions often found it hard to understand one another. All the same, there were many common features in their lives which make it possible to attempt a general description of a mining village.

Thus, although the character of pit villages varied greatly, they were generally unlovely in setting and appearance. The colliery was often just a few yards away, and the immediate landscape was dominated by mountainous waste-tips thrown up by years of screening. The size of the tips was such that, at Aberfan in 1966, when one tip became unstable and slid into a nearby stream, the resulting mudflow instantly engulfed the local primary school and several village houses, killing 144 people – mostly children.

Colliers' houses were, more often than not, built by the mine-owners during the nineteenth century. This was the only way a substantial workforce could be accommodated when new pits were being opened up, and incidentally gave the owners an extra means of controlling the colliers, who were only allowed to carry on renting their houses while they were employed by the company; a man who became discontented and left the pit had to find a new home for himself and his family. (A similar 'tied cottage' system prevailed in farming.) The houses varied greatly in size and amenities, depending on the date at which they were built. Even in the 1940s, at Backworth:

There were some of the old pit cottages, built by the mine-owners. They were rather poor one-up one-down brick cottages. (*Frank Crosland*)

43

35 *A collier and his family, evicted from their home during a strike in 1891*

36 *Colliers' houses at Twizell*

But most were probably better than that – two-up two-down houses with a parlour/sitting-room and a kitchen on the ground floor and a couple of bedrooms above them. Some might also have a tiny scullery and a scrap of garden. There would be no bathroom, an outside WC, and possibly no running water except for a communal tap out in the street.

Many of these houses were in fact soundly built, and represented a great improvement on earlier miners' dwellings; at the turn of the twentieth century there were still old men alive who remembered the days when these consisted only of a single-roomed cottage for an entire family. But, in time, the Victorian houses also came to be seen as inadequate. New amenities arrived only slowly in mining villages, and during the long stagnant era between the World Wars many once-sound buildings deteriorated. By the 1940s the housing of miners was recognized as a national scandal.

Even at its best, the pit village struck outsiders as a dreary place, with not much more than chapels, pubs and a few shops to break the monotony of the colliers' houses, which were uniformly and unimaginatively laid out. A single-occupation village had no variety and no roots in history:

Bowers Row . . . would certainly not have qualified for the National Trust. It had no beautiful stone-built cottages, no ancient church, no historic background; just three hundred red-brick houses in long grubby rows.

(Jim Bullock, *Them and Us*)

A man's world

At home, the miner – like many working-class people – spent much of his time in the kitchen, preferring its cosiness to the grandeur of the parlour, which tended to be reserved for formal visits, piano lessons and laying out family corpses before funerals. There was always a good fire going in the kitchen – one advantage of being a miner was that you got your coal free, or very cheap. When he came home from work, the collier usually ate first, then stripped off in front of

37 *A miner's wife pours water into a tin bath so that her husband can wash. Even in 1947, when the mines were nationalized, many colliers were without adequate washing facilities at work and at home.*

the fire with a tub of hot water and scrubbed off the pit-dirt, getting his wife to do his back. The pit bleached his skin – so much so that, as D.H. Lawrence noticed, even after they had been 'out' for four months in 1926, Eastwood colliers could still be identified by their pallor.

Colliers had other distinctive features. One was their walk, 'the lurching, almost slinking walk of colliers, swinging their heavy feet and going as if the mine-roof were still over their heads' (D.H. Lawrence, 'Return to Bestwood'). Another was their habit of squatting when waiting or conversing in a group; Lawrence recorded it in the Midlands, and, as late as the Second World War, in the North-East: 'The old miners didn't

38 *Colliers with a champion whippet. Whippet-racing was a particularly popular sport in mining communities.*

stand, they'd sort of squat on their heels, even when they were on the surface.' (Frank Crosland)

The mining village was very much a traditional, male-dominated society. Working together in difficult conditions, the colliers developed a cult of manliness and an exceptional camaraderie that overflowed into their lives outside the pit – a rather curious by-product of the enlightened legislation that forbade the employment of women underground. Since the relative isolation and specialized nature of the pit village meant that there were few opportunities for women to work, the man remained the exclusive 'bread-winner' to a greater extent than elsewhere; and this also had its effect. The man didn't help about the house, though he might do a little cobbling or beer-brewing if he had the knack. All sorts of activities were considered 'unmanly'; Lawrence was amazed in 1926 to see colliers blackberrying, an occupation they would normally have regarded as beneath their dignity. In many households, if there were wages to be divided among the men who worked together at a stall, the woman had to leave the room; she was not supposed to know what her husband earned.

Such attitudes were not confined to the colliers, but they were more emphatically held and slower to change here than elsewhere. This was also true of leisure-time activities: men tended to congregate together, and after working in the closed world of the pit a good many of them enjoyed rough-and-ready pleasures, as Frank Crosland recalls:

A rather turbulent community, you know. Pit, then up to the club for boozing, then come out

FRED DOWSON,
"1ST PRIZE WINNER
HORSE & GROOM"
LEEK SHOW, 1916,
CASTLESIDE.

39 *Gardening, the outdoor hobby, understandably appealed to men who spent their working lives underground.*

on a Saturday night and have a good old fight with somebody, and perhaps two days later they'd be quite good friends again . . . . Often they'd keep the gelignite in a tin under the bed: no sense of security! They were great gamblers too. Training whippets and racing pigeons, that was another thing colliers were famous for. And they were keen gardeners, those who worked on night shifts.

Still, miners of the late nineteenth and early twentieth centuries were less wild than their fore-

fathers. Some of this may have been the result of Board School education – the elementary education provided by the state from about the 1870s. But 'chapel' – Nonconformity – was probably a more important influence. Neglected by the Established Church (the Church of England), pit villages in most parts of Britain took to Methodism and other Nonconformist creeds. 'Chapel' combined evangelical fervour with insistence on respectable behaviour, the promotion of self-help and a marked radical strain. (British socialism has often been described as springing mainly from the Nonconformist tradition.) It could be oppressive, making things difficult for people who would not conform to Nonconformity, but overall it made an undeniable contribution to the morale of mining folk. Among other things, chapels were the main social centres of the villages (apart from the pubs), and Sunday School, the Band of Hope temperance association, debating societies and similar chapel-based activities assumed an importance in people's lives that we can now hardly appreciate.

Injury, disease and death

The mining village was a close-knit community, often rather suspicious of outsiders. But among themselves, the miners and their families practised a good deal of mutual aid. Frank Crosland noticed that 'When anyone was in trouble they'd help them out'; and it was this tradition of mutual support that enabled miners to sustain strikes for such extraordinarily long periods. Community spirit was kept alive by shared misfortune, and every mining family had to live with the constant fear or knowledge of death. The worst moments, inevitably, were after something went wrong underground, when wives, relatives and friends would maintain a grim pithead vigil, hoping with increasing desperation that the menfolk would be brought up alive. The last major underground disasters of the twentieth century were in 1934, at Gresford in Denbighshire, when 265 men were killed in a terrible explosion, and in 1947, when 104 died at

40 *A colliery band celebrates the nationalization of the mines in January 1947. The brass band is one of the great traditional institutions of mining communities.*

Whitehaven's William Pit in Cumberland; but smaller tragedies have continued to occur right down to the present day. Even in years when there was no disaster, fatal accidents were common (858 in 1938); some were 'true' accidents, scarcely avoidable, but the sharp fall in numbers after nationalization indicates that inadequate precautions and bad conditions were largely to blame.

Apart from bereavements, other wounds inflicted by the mines could be seen in every pit village. There were the injured and mutilated – a man with a foot crushed by a rock fall, or perhaps a couple of fingers taken off by the cutter chain. And there were the sick. Mining was at best an unhealthy occupation. Men suffered from swollen 'beat' knees, the joints inflamed by crawling on all

fours or kneeling and shovelling for hours; knee-pads offered only limited protection, since small pieces of stone easily worked their way between knee and pad, adding to the discomfort and irritation. Until the 1930s the dim lighting underground caused nystagmus, an extra-ordinary, painful disease in which the victim's eyeballs oscillated strangely and uncontrollably, causing temporary blindness. Worst of all was pneumoconiosis – 'black lung disease' – which first took away the breath of men in their prime, then made them aged and skeletal, and finally killed them long before their time. It was a disease specific to coalmining, caused by a build-up of dust particles eating into the lung tissue. It was, and is, a singularly cruel and incapacitating affliction.

The managers

There was one other presence in the mining village: the management. Relations between the management and colliers' families were often

surprisingly 'feudal' especially down to the early twentieth century. The colliery manager might live in a big house in or just outside the village, employing the miners' daughters as domestic servants and taking the lead on Sundays at chapel. As we have seen, most miners lived in

41 *Rescue workers digging beneath a shattered school roof at Aberfan in Wales. In October 1966 a collapsed waste-tip (its size can be gauged from illustration 33) engulfed a school and houses, killing 144 people – the worst mining-related disaster for decades.*

tied houses; and the smallness of the community meant that their activities were well-known to the managers. Bill Haywood remembers the days before nationalization:

Well, they [the managers] were rotten before then. If I had a son and didn't take him to Moorgreen, they would come out of their offices and say, 'Your son's leaving school, isn't he? Bring him down!'

This was perhaps an extreme case, but bad feeling between management and men was certainly not; as it intensified between the wars it became much less common for managers to live in the pit villages. For the most part, the managers were simply carrying out the owners' wishes when they 'kept the men in their place'. Even a progressive manager like Jim Bullock was helpless when his boss turned up and put on an elaborate act to avoid making improvements or paying extra allowances – an act that might include wiping the sweat off his face and putting on a thick scarf before entering the hottest part of the pit, thus 'proving' that the ventilation was much better than it had been! Of the period 1930-8, Bullock says simply: 'There was more trickery, more deliberate lying, more deceiving during this period than at any other.'

Nationalization changed many things, and in the decades after the Second World War the miners themselves changed. The majority, like the majority of British people, gradually stopped attending churches and chapels except for marriages, christenings and funerals. They became steadily better off. Radio from the 1930s, and television from the 1950s, brought them into closer touch with the rest of the world. Owning a car made it easier to visit larger towns and possible to live further from work, which also meant away from the pit village. And with successive reorganizations of the industry, many miners were forced to leave their native areas and fit into new communities. In other words, miners gradually became more like everybody else. And yet, to a surprising extent, the pit village has survived, and with it many of the old attitudes and values.

5 Switchback: The Mines Since Nationalization

'A new world'

1 January 1947 was 'Vesting Day' – the day on which the British coal mines were taken into public ownership under the control of the National Coal Board (NCB). This was a day that the miners had looked forward to for over 30 years, and there were speeches and celebrations as the NCB flag was run up at each pit. Brand-new notices proclaimed that 'This colliery is now managed by the National Coal Board on behalf of the People.' Coal was to be only the first of several industries nationalized by the Labour Government of 1945-50, which had been swept to power on a promise to reconstruct society and prevent a return of 'the bad old days' before the war.

In mining, as in other things, many of the brightest hopes were not realized. The early post-war years – the 'Austerity Period' – were hard and uncomfortable, and heavy demands were made on the miners; during and after the savage winter of 1946-7 they found themselves working as relentlessly in the national interest as they had once worked for private owners. Nationalization, too, brought disappointments. The government and NCB had a healthy respect for the National Union of Mineworkers (NUM), the powerful national union which had replaced the old Federation in 1945. But the workers had no significant say in the actual running of the mines, which – as they saw it – were handed over to a suspect combination of old managers and new bureaucrats. And the NCB, although nominally independent, was, in reality, controlled by successive governments of varying political

42 *Vesting Day. On 1 January 1947 notices like this went up at collieries all over Britain, proclaiming that the mines had been nationalized and would in future be run by the National Coal Board.*

outlooks which pulled it in different directions. The industry was sometimes supposed to be 'serving the nation' regardless of profit and loss; at other times it was told to operate 'like a proper business'; and quite often it was implicitly expected to do both at the same time. Additional uncertainties were created by the fluctuations in the demand for coal over four decades, which led to 'switchback' policies in which the industry alternately prospered and declined, contracted and expanded.

All the same, nationalization transformed the industry in its first ten years. It would be very difficult to find a miner who disagreed with Jeffrey Jennings's verdict:

NCB made a lot of difference, you know. When NCB took over, it were a new world. It was a good thing . . .

There was an enormous demand for coal at home and abroad, and the government was prepared to invest heavily to get it. A rapid, full-scale mechanization was undertaken at last. New machines, which cut *all* the coal *and* loaded it, were introduced wherever feasible; eventually there were several models of cutter-loader, able to deal with seams of every width. Haulage roads were straightened and widened so that conveyor belts or trains could bring the coal all the way from the face to the pit bottom. 'Manriding' trains saved time and effort by carrying miners to and from the face. Wooden pit-props were replaced

---

43 *'Manriding' trains such as this one, at Yorkshire's Kiveton Park Colliery, now take colliers to and from the coal face. In the past, colliers walked – or got an illicit and dangerous 'lift', as in illustration 21.*

44 *A radio-controlled coal-cutting 'shearer' at Yorkshire's Kellingley Colliery*

by steel, and later still by self-advancing hydraulic chocks, which meant that cutting and loading the coal and supporting the roof could go on almost without a break. Finally, to come to recent years, machines – 'boom rippers' – were introduced to drive the tunnels through coal or rock.

In the early years after nationalization many worked-out, inefficient, old pits were closed; but thanks to modernization and the opening of new pits, there were jobs for all. In fact, there was a shortage of men to work in the mines, and the age of the workforce was looked on as a source of worry: of 690,000 miners, 350,000 were over 40, and a vigorous recruitment campaign was needed to bring the total numbers back above 700,000.

The improvement in conditions above and below ground was dramatic. Training schemes, holidays with pay and proper insurance and compensation arrangements regularized the collier's existence. Pithead baths, still only provided at half the collieries of Britain on Vesting Day, rapidly became universal. The 140,000 company-owned miners' dwellings had been purchased by the government along with the mines themselves, and from then onwards housing conditions were substantially improved.

In many small but important ways – for example, by providing tools instead of expecting the workforce to buy them – the NCB was a far better employer than the colliery companies had ever been. Attempts were made to alleviate the menace of dust in the air, which machines made worse; the machines were sprayed with water, dust masks were issued, and, eventually, an airstream helmet was devised which incorporated a fan that directed filtered air across the

miner's face. Although the mines never became a positively healthy place, stricter observance of safety regulations and other improvements brought down rapidly the rate of accidents and fatalities. There were 618 deaths in 1947 and 420 in 1952; by 1979-80, with an admittedly smaller workforce, the figure was down to 30.

On the switchback

In the 1950s British mines were producing over 200 million tons of coal a year, and still failing to keep up with demand. An important reason for this was that governments deliberately kept the price low, encouraging the post-war recovery of industry by providing it with cheap fuel. Miners were well paid, yet it proved hard to recruit

45 *The Titan Tunneller, used to drive 'roads' (tunnels) through to the coal face. This one is at Warsop Colliery in Derbyshire.*

were well paid, yet it proved hard to recruit enough of them; there were good, clean, reasonably paid jobs to be had elsewhere, and the NCB's assurances that a miner had 'a job for life' carried only limited weight in a full-employment society.

Then came the 'down' on the switchback – a complete reversal of the situation which began to be obvious in 1957, as stockpiles of unsold coal began to accumulate. It was realized – rather late in the day – that large sections of industry were converting to oil, which was cheaper than coal and in plentiful supply, while nuclear power was widely seen as the fuel of the more distant future. Demand for coal fell, and both Conservative and Labour governments responded by closing down mines and employing fewer men, paying little or no attention to warnings that dependence on cheap foreign oil might be dangerous. By 1970 the workforce was down to 300,000, and only 293 pits were left – a change of massive proportions. The areas that suffered most were the older ones – the North-East, Scotland and South Wales – where the seams were thinner and productivity per man was, therefore, lower; but a surprising number of recently opened pits, representing heavy investments, were also axed. These were 'uneconomic' pits – that is, pits that did not make a profit in the circumstances of the moment. But, unlike the pits closed as a result of nationalization, they were not worked-out, and their loss was later regretted. (When a coal mine is closed and not continuously maintained, it soon collapses on itself and cannot be re-opened.) Since there was still full employment, the men who left mining generally did so for good, often moving right away from the coalfields. Those who carried on were less well-paid, as least in relative terms. Almost everyone was becoming better-off during the 1960s, but the miners dropped behind many other groups in the 'league table' of wages, since their claims were met with the argument that higher wages put up the price of coal, making it less competitive and costing still more jobs. Almost the only positive step during these years

46 *Despite great improvements in safety standards, mining remains a dangerous occupation. Here rescue workers wrapped in blankets return to the surface after the Lofthouse Colliery disaster in March 1973.*

was the abolition (1965) of the old piece-work price-list and the introduction of a uniform daily wage. There were fears that lack of incentives would diminish productivity, and although these proved unfounded, a bonus scheme was later (1978) introduced.

Eventually the miners revolted, and in 1969 unofficial strikes started in Yorkshire and spread to other British coalfields. As well as gaining concessions over hours and wages, the strikes showed that the long period of co-operation between miners and NCB had come to an end. The NUM itself became increasingly militant, and won victories in the national strikes of 1972 and 1974; in 1974 the government's mishandling of the strike effectively led to its electoral defeat and loss of office.

One reason why the miners' bargaining position had grown so much stronger was that the switchback had made another change of direction. The oil-producing countries, acting together through their OPEC organization, shook loose from Western influence and raised the

47   *A superb picture, taken in 1955 by the famous* Picture Post *photographer Bert Hardy. It represents an experiment in combating underground fires by driving a wall of foam in front of the fire-fighters; the foam was created by mixing detergent and water and forcing the bubbles through a mesh. The photograph was taken in a specially built model 'mine'.*

price of their products very steeply. Suddenly coal was cheaper – 'economic' – again, and the government began re-investing and urging the opening of new mines. By the late 1970s a new 'supermine' – actually a linked group of collieries – had opened at Selby in Yorkshire, and plans were being laid for another in the Vale of Belvoir in Leicestershire.

But, by this time, circumstances had changed again. By the 1980s Britain was in a trough of recession, with well over three million people unemployed. Though long-term prospects for coal still looked good, the effects of the recession were inevitably felt. Notable among these were

48 *Miners demonstrating in 1974. The victorious strike in that year brought down the government and represented the culmination of several years' growing militancy.*

the rapid decline of the steel industry, which had been a big coal consumer, a decreased demand for electricity by the nation's flagging industries, competition from foreign coal producers and the deposits of natural gas and oil discovered in the North Sea. At the same time the government was insisting that the NCB should become a profitable concern, which, in practice, meant another round of pit closures. Government redundancy payments, accepted by most older men, eased the process; the younger men at 'uneconomic' pits were transferred elsewhere.

By 1984 the number of men employed in mining was down to 196,000. Thanks to redundancies, it was a young workforce, in complete contrast to the situation in the 1940s. But, by 1984, redundancy payments had less appeal to the younger miners, since, given the high level of unemployment, it seemed likely that they might never find another job, and might have to spend the rest of their lives in decaying workless communities. The government's plans seemed ultimately to envisage shutting down the entire coal industry in areas such as the North-East and South Wales, and concentrating on the newer pits of Yorkshire and the Midlands, with their thick, straight, highly productive seams. The miners protested that billions of tons of coal would be lost, and communities destroyed, by such a policy. The government pointed out the heavy cost to the taxpayer of maintaining the older pits, and also committed itself to an ambitious nuclear power programme to meet future energy requirements.

In this conflict between utterly different philosophies, genuine agreement seemed out of the question. In 1981 the government introduced a new programme of closures but was forced to back down. In 1984, more favourably placed, it tried again. The result was extraordinary – a national strike that lasted for no less than a year, during which the courts ordered the seizure of union funds, violence flared again and again between police and strikers, and protracted negotiations produced no results. The strike of 1984-5 indicated that, for all the changes of the previous 40 years, the miners were still not quite like any other workers; and that the pit villages (at times, during the strike, in a virtual state of siege) were still distinctive communities.

In March 1985 the miners at last gave up the strike and returned to work. New closures now seemed certain; but after so many ups and downs on the switchback it would be rash to predict the future development of the industry.

The miner of today – and tomorrow?

Mechanization and modern technology have made most miners technicians – machine drivers or operatives, fitters, electricians and engineers (plus of course deputies, surveyors, nursing officers, coal preparation staff, administrators etc.). But working in a mine is still not comparable to working on the factory floor or even on a building site. It is cramped, dirty, and, usually, hot. Even at a showpiece colliery such as Bevercotes in Nottinghamshire, with its air-conditioning, thick seams and advanced machinery, the face-worker takes off his NCB overalls and still works in shorts and singlet; he still has to crawl to get through to the cutter he operates, still gets scratched and bruised, and still – like other underground workers – comes up filthy to the surface. Despite airstream helmets and masks, dust remains an affliction and a health hazard. The ripper is still at risk as he sounds and supports the machine-cut roof, which is as unpredictable as ever. In fact, geology has not been mastered; well-advertised attempts to make mining an entirely remote-controlled operation at Bevercotes failed when a fault in the seam threw everything awry. Though many operations are being computerized by MINOS (the Mine Operating System), it is questionable whether mining will ever be a 'white collar' job.

The Wilberforce Court of Inquiry, set up to

---

49 *Miners demonstrating during the year-long strike of 1984-5. As a result of redundancy schemes they are now mostly young men – much younger on average than the miners of even ten years before, seen in illustration 48.*

arbitrate in the dispute of 1972, found that the miners were 'a special case', since:

Other occupations have their dangers and inconveniences, but we know of none other in which there is such a combination of danger, health hazard, discomfort in working conditions, social inconvenience and community isolation.

For some time to come, at least, mining is likely to remain 'a special case'.

50 *Miners' wives jeer at 'scabs' who carried on working during the strike of 1984-5. For the first time, women played an important part in a coal-mining dispute. The strike divided the miners, and accusations of picket-line and police violence further embittered matters.*

Date List

1698	Thomas Savery's steam engine, advertised as 'the miner's friend' because it could be used to pump water from the pits
1708	Thomas Newcomen improves on Savery's steam engine
1769	James Watt patents his condenser, a decisive improvement to the steam engine
1799-1800	Combination Acts suppress trade unions
1815	Safety lamp invented by Davy and others
1824	Repeal of Combination Acts
1835	Wallsend Colliery disaster: 102 killed; parliamentary enquiry into mine disasters
1842	Mines Act, barring women, and children under ten, from working underground: first state regulation of coalmining
1843	First government inspector of mines appointed (but with no authority to go underground until 1850)
1860s	Introduction of first ventilating fans
1862	Minimum of two shafts made compulsory for every colliery after Hartley Pit disaster, in which 204 men suffocate
1872	Act of Parliament makes training and certificate compulsory for colliery managers
1880s	First uses of electricity underground
1889	Miners' Federation of Great Britain formed
1893	300,000 Federation miners on strike for five months against 25 per cent cut in wages
1894	Coal Mines Act makes first arrangements for checkweighmen
1895-1900	Earliest coal-cutting machines introduced

1905	First conveyor belts used
1908	Act limiting miner's shift to eight hours
1910	Worst year for fatal accidents in British coal mines: 1818 killed
1912	First national strike (a million men out for seven weeks) secures Minimum Wage Act
1913	Worst-ever disaster, at Universal Colliery, Sengenhydd, Glamorgan: 439 killed
	Highest-ever output of coal achieved: 287,430,473 tons
1919	Sankey Report: majority recommend nationalization
1921	National strike lasting three months
1926	Samuel Commission; General Strike; miners stay out for six months
1930	Coal Mines Act to fix production quotas and prices, and to encourage amalgamations
1932	41 per cent of coal mine-workers unemployed
1934	Gresford Colliery disaster: 265 killed
1945	National Union of Mineworkers (NUM) formed
1947	Nationalization of the coal mines. William Pit disaster: 104 killed
1966	Aberfan disaster: 144 people (116 children) killed when colliery waste-tip engulfs village houses and school
1972	National strike and Wilberforce Court of Inquiry
1974	National strike; fall of Edward Heath's government
Late 1970s	Selby, first of the 'supermines', opened
1979	Golbourne Colliery disaster: 10 killed
1984-5	Year-long national strike against NCB plans for colliery closures
1985	Non-strikers break with NUM and form a rival union

Glossary

bell-pit primitive method of mining which involved sinking a shaft down to the coal seam and then hewing the coal out from the shaft bottom in a rough circle; when the circle was so large that the roof might fall in, the pit was simply abandoned. Also known as a beehive pit

Bevin boys Instead of being conscripted into the armed forces during the Second World War, 20,000 young men were sent into the coal mines; they were called 'Bevin boys' after the Minister of Labour, Ernest Bevin.

brazier movable vessel used to hold hot coals

butty The 'big' butty was a middleman between the mine-owners and the colliers; he contracted to produce a fixed quantity of coal by a given date – a system that encouraged slave-driving of the colliers. The big butty disappeared during the nineteenth century, but in some places the 'little' butty survived into the twentieth. This kind of butty was an experienced collier who took charge of a particular 'stall' at the coal face. He was paid for all the coal won at his stall, and in turn paid his hired helpers, who were often members of his family.

cage lift that carries men and materials up and down a pit shaft

checkweighman person employed by the colliers to check that the amount of coal each man (or team) had won was correctly weighed and recorded by the employers

Davy lamp safety lamp invented by Sir Humphrey Davy in 1815. Its principal feature was a gauze surround that absorbed the heat generated by the lamp; there was therefore no explosion if the lamp came into contact with combustible gas and air mixtures. This ceased to be true if a strong draught upset the evenness of the absorption; and the lamp had various other drawbacks.

deputy mine official, responsible for safety underground

inbye underground, a route leading away from the shaft, towards the face

laissez-faire the dominant economic philosophy during the nineteenth century; occasionally revived, with modifications, since then. It argued that economic processes (or 'market forces') worked best if state interference was kept to a minimum. This was one reason given for resistance to Factory Acts controlling child labour, safety, hours of work, etc.

lime-burning an important British occupation for centuries. The lime-burner in fact burned limestone in order to make lime, which was widely used to improve the quality of agricultural land.

longwall method of working coal seams by advancing the entire coal face in a continuous line (i.e. in one long wall). Only the immediate working area is supported; as the face advances, the worked-out waste area behind the colliers is allowed to collapse.

nystagmus disease which caused the eyeballs to move about strangely, and led to temporary blindness. It was mainly found among underground workers who operated in inadequate lighting.

outbye underground, a route leading away from the face, towards the shaft

overburden general term for the entire thickness of rock lying above a coal seam

pillar and stall method of working coal that involved tunneling into the seam, leaving uncut pillars of coal to support the roof. Longwall (q.v.) has been more common in Britain for well over a century.

pit bottom area round the base of a shaft, from which the miner walks or rides out to the face

pithead surface area of a colliery – buildings, plant and machinery

pneumoconiosis disease of the lung tissues, caused by the action of coal dust

ripper miner whose job is to enlarge and support the roofs or roadways, creating room for haulage and other operations

road underground tunnel; also known as a gate

screening plant place where the coal is separated from waste material and graded according to size

smelting heating an ore so that the metal content melts and can be run off: a major use for coal during the Industrial Revolution

snap collier's term for the meal he brings underground with him; it is carried in a snap tin

soup kitchen place where soups or similar foods are prepared and given out in quantities to the destitute, the unemployed, strikers or other people in difficulties. Soup kitchens are generally set up by charities, or by the organization representing the group concerned.

stall section of a coal face allocated to a particular collier or team

tommy shop shop operating on the truck system (q.v.). Because their customers could not buy elsewhere, the tommy shops notoriously sold inferior goods at inflated prices.

tram another word for tub (q.v.)

trapping opening and shutting ventilation doors for wagons to pass through. The trapper was usually a child, even in the early twentieth century.

truck system by which wages were not paid in cash but in goods – most commonly in credits which could only be spent at tommy shops (q.v.) belonging to the employers

tub small open vehicle, running on rails and used to transport coal underground

Vesting Day 1 January 1947, the day on which Britain's coal mines were nationalized

waste area underground from which the coal has been removed; also known as the gob or goaf

Books for Further Reading

D. Anderson, *Coal: A Pictorial History of the British Coal Industry*, David and Charles, 1982

Israel Berkovitch, *Coal on the Switchback: The Coal Industry since Nationalization*, Allan and Unwin, 1977

Hugh Bodey, *Past into Present Mining*, Batsford, 1976

Jim Bullock, *Them and Us*, Souvenir Press, 1972

David Day, *The Bevin Boy*, Roundwood Press, 1975

Dave Douglass and Jack Krieger, *A Miner's Life*, Routledge, 1983

Tony Hall, *King Coal: Miners, Coal and Britain's Industrial Future*, Penguin, 1981

Norman Harrison, *Once a Miner*, Oxford University Press, 1954

D.H. Lawrence, 'Return to Bestwood'. Essay written in 1926. Book publication in *Phoenix II*, 1968; more widely available in *A Selection from Phoenix* (ed. A.A.H. Inglis), Peregrine Books, 1971

George Orwell, *The Road to Wigan Pier*, Gollancz, 1937 (available in Penguin)

Peter Pagnamenta and Richard Overy, *All Our Working Lives*, BBC, 1984

Will Paynter, *My Generation*, Allen and Unwin, 1972

Michael Pollard, *The Hardest Work Under Heaven: The Life and Death of the British Coal Miner*, Hutchinson, 1984

Bernard Taylor (Lord Taylor of Mansfield), *Uphill All the Way: A Miner's Struggle*, Sidgwick and Jackson, 1972

Interesting picture books include Phillipa Aston and Chris Fairclough, *A Day with a Miner*, Wayland, 1981, and W. Birtles, *Working at a Coal Mine*, Wayland, 1982.

Fiction
Specially recommended and widely available novels:

D.H. Lawrence, *Sons and Lovers*, Duckworth, 1913

Richard Llewelyn, *How Green Was My Valley*

Emile Zola (translated by L.W. Tancock), *Germinal*, Penguin, 1954

Index